LIST OF PLATES

HENRI DE TOULOUSE-LAUTREC

1864-1901

The myth of the artist as tortured soul, isolated by his genius from normal relationships, is nowhere more comprehensively indulged than in the popular view of Henri de Toulouse-Lautrec. John Huston's classic biopic, *Moulin Rouge* (1952), starring Jose Ferrer, portrays the artist as both emotionally and physically stunted. His life is depicted as a series of fleeting and unsatisfactory love affairs, and his art as a compensatory creative outlet for social inadequacy.

It is perhaps inevitable that such an account should prove to be an over-simplification, not only of the artist's life but of his work. His family was an ancient one, and he remained on reasonably good terms with his parents, who supported him in the early stages of his career. His mother moved with him to Paris in 1872, when he was eight, so that he could attend the prestigious Lycée Fontanes, continuing to provide a home for him after his decision to train as an artist. It was his father, however, himself deeply interested in art and with a wide range of artist friends, who first introduced Lautrec to the bohemian world that was to become his life and livelihood. In that world Lautrec made many loyal and devoted friends, who provided him with the support and security that he seemed desperately to need. One, who studied with him from 1882 at the studio of Fernand Cormon, described him thus:

His most striking characteristics, it seemed to me, were his outstanding intelligence and constant alertness, his abundant good will towards his devoted friends, and his profound understanding of his fellow men.

It is not unusual for those suffering from some obvious disability to be more concerned with putting others at their ease than with overt expressions of sympathy, and Lautrec seems to have been remarkable for his humor, wit and charm. Thadée Natanson, a long-standing friend, said simply: 'It required enormous effort to see him as he appeared to the rest of the world.'

If the notion of Lautrec as social outcast appears an exaggeration, to view his art as simply a record of the cafe and cabaret life of fin-de siècle Paris would be correspondingly an over-simplification. The tough, seamy, proletarian world that Lautrec inhabited and portrayed – the bars, cafés and theaters, the dancers, shopgirls and prostitutes – had also been the province of those Impressionists, such as Pissarro and Degas, who regarded the urban as well as the rural environment as suitable subject-matter for the artist. Degas was the living artist for whom Lautrec had the greatest respect and affection, and his debt to him is considerable, both in terms of subject-matter and style. Technical borrowings include the cropping of images, the snapshot-like presentation of subjects and the use of lighting from below. But while Degas presents a detached view of his anonymous subjects, who are described in the titles of his paintings simply by their role – orchestral player, laundress, milliner – Lautrec gives his subjects names, individuality, a personal identity, even to the point of caricature. The critic Robert Hughes has hailed his 'precocious modernity', his 'caustic and tender view of the world', and it is just this ambiguous combination of satire and sympathy that gives Lautrec's work its particular force and quality.

Henri Marie Raymond de Toulouse-Lautrec-Monfa was born on 24 November, 1864, at the family home in Albi, the Hotel du Bosc. His father, Comte Alphonse Charles de Toulouse-Lautrec, was descended from a junior branch of the family of the counts of Toulouse, who had been fervent crusaders and defenders of the true faith against the Albigensian heresy in the twelfth century. His mother, Adèle-Zoë Tapié de Céleyran, came from a wealthy but much more recently ennobled family. This aristocratic lineage, in an increasingly democratic and industrialized society where the aristocracy led an enclosed and relatively powerless existence, provided a particular social and cultural context in which the young Henri was raised. His flamboyant father compensated for the disparity between the splendid family history and its present political insignificance with an eccentricity that bordered on the unbalanced. His two main pastimes were hunting and dressing up; he had a complete wardrobe of costumes in which he had himself photographed, and once descended for lunch dressed in a plaid and a ballet-dancer's tutu. His son shared both his disdain for convention and his contempt for the bourgeoisie, but in Lautrec's case this brought him into sympathy with the working class, and with the Anarchist movement that was a feature of late nineteenth-century Europe.

Like many noble families, the Toulouse-Lautrecs' family tree was fruitful with intermarriages. Lautrec's grandmothers were sisters, his parents first cousins. His father's sister married his mother's brother, and three of their 14 children suffered birth defects, one of them being a dwarf. There seems little doubt that Lautrec himself suffered from *Pycnodysostosis*, a rare genetic bone disorder linked with parental consanguinity. This usually becomes apparent at adolescence, when the arms and legs cease to grow at the same rate as the rest of the body. Throughout his life, Lautrec remained just under five feet tall, with a normally-sized head and torso but short legs and knock knees. Other symptoms of the disease which marked him were unusually large nostrils, a receding chin, protuberant red lips, and an enlarged tongue which made him lisp and salivate excessively. When the music-hall singer Yvette Guilbert first met him, she noted 'the huge, dark head, the red face and black beard, the greasy, oily skin, the nose broad enough for two faces, and a mouth that gashed the face from cheek to cheek, with huge violet-rose lips that were at once flat and flaccid.' Then, however, she noticed his eyes: 'Oh, how fine, large, richly warm and astonishingly bright they were!'

Lautrec's earliest years were divided between the Albi town house and the family chateaux of Bosc, north of Albi, and Céleyran, near Narbonne. His mother, a quiet and pious woman, seems to have remained devoted to him; she became estranged from her husband when Lautrec was about five, and there were no other surviving children. With the move to Paris in 1872, Lautrec was introduced to the artistic side of his inheritance. His grandfather had been an accomplished draftsman, his uncle Charles was a keen amateur artist, who encouraged the boy's earliest attempts to draw, and his father both drew and painted. Two accidents in 1878 and 1879, in which Lautrec broke first the left and then the right leg, made him a semi-invalid for a couple of years and gave him the opportunity to practice and improve his already considerable drawing skills. This period, marked by a series of painful operations and other medical devices intending to improve his mobility, also reinforced the self-deprecating humor and courage with which he faced his disabilities; in March 1878 he wrote to his grandmother about yet another operation: 'On Monday the surgical crime was committed, and the fracture, so interesting from the surgical point of view (but not, needless to say, from mine) was revealed . . . '

Comte Alphonse's favorite painter was René Princeteau (1839-1914), a deaf mute famous for his paintings of horses, who became, on an informal basis, Lautrec's first instructor. Lautrec was himself a keen rider from the age of four, a strong swimmer, and an inveterate party-goer. His earliest drawings are mainly of falcons, horses and herons. In 1875 he left the Lycée Fontanes and, for the next six years, divided his time between Albi and Céleyran, with occasional visits to Paris. This largely rural environment produced the only landscapes he painted, the last one dating from 1881, when he finally decided to become an artist. From the beginning, his real interest was in portraiture, the communication by brush and pen of the quirks of individual character.

Lautrec's parents made no objection to his becoming a gentleman artist, there being no necessity for him to earn a living, and under Princeteau's guidance he was accepted into the studio of Léon Bonnat (1833-1922), a fashionable portrait painter whose almost photographic realism earned him a large clientele. Bonnat laid great stress on drawing, and much of Lautrec's time with him was spent in copying classical models. When Bonnat gave up private tuition in the summer of 1882, Lautrec moved to the studio of Fernand Cormon (1845-1924), describing him in a letter to his father as a 'powerful, austere and original talent'.

For the first 18 months of his apprenticeship with Cormon, Lautrec continued to live with his mother in the family apartment near the Faubourg St-Honoré, but the artistic and social environment that he found at Cormon's soon provided an alternative family. Among the more formidable talents to study there were Emile Bernard, Vincent van Gogh and Louis Anquetin, the last of whom was responsible for introducing Lautrec to Aristide Bruant. The influence of Manet and the Impressionists on Lautrec's work is clearest in these early years, before his own characteristic style was fully developed, but already his fascination with the popular illustrated press, the social satire and the political caricature spawned by rapid industrialization and social change, was a clear feature of his work. The caricaturist Honoré Daumier (1808-79), who produced over 4000 lithographs for a variety of journals and was an ardent republican, was a particularly strong influence. Lautrec also admired the paintings and illustrations of Jean-Louis Forain (1852-1931), whom, like Princeteau, he met through his father. Forain was both painter and caricaturist, exhibiting work in four of the Impressionist exhibitions. His blurring of the boundaries between Fine Art and illustration laid the basis for much of Lautrec's mature work.

Another element in Lautrec's development while working with Cormon, one that he shared with many of his contemporaries as well as with the Impressionists, was his interest in all things Japanese, and above all Japanese woodblock prints. Where his father had himself photographed as a Highland chief, Lautrec was portrayed as a samurai, and in 1886 he and van Gogh discussed the possibility of traveling to Japan together. It is in his graphic art that this Japanese influence can be most clearly traced; in his dramatic organization of space, the use of flat areas of pure color and clearly defined contour lines, and the emphasis on decorative patterns.

Between the mid 1880s and about 1891, Lautrec's art focused on two main themes. The largest body of work is devoted to portraiture, while a smaller group portrays the nocturnal social life of Montmartre. In 1884 Lautrec, aged 20, had left the family apartment and taken up lodgings with René Grenier, another Cormon student, and his wife Lily. Throughout his time in Paris, Lautrec lived and worked within a small area in Montmartre, which had been a village outside Paris until included within the mid-nineteenth-century fortifications built by Louis-Philippe, the citizen king. Situated on a hill, with Baron Haussmann's great boulevards of the 1860s at its feet, Montmartre in the 1880s was still self-consciously distinct from Paris proper and had acquired the status of refuge for those who, for one reason or another, were disinclined to conform to the pressures of an increasingly industrialized society.

Montmartre was also the common element in Lautrec's painting of the 1880s. One of his first models outside the circle of family and friends who provided his earliest subjects was a young laundress, Carmen Gaudin, a working-class girl whom he met in the street in 1885. Working-class women had become a popular subject in French art, adopted as the heroines of modern life by such contemporary Realist writers as Zola and the Goncourt brothers, and Montmartre, with its population of small tradesfolk and entertainers, as well as less reputable professions, provided little else.

Montmartre also proved fertile ground for the growing number of magazines and journals catering to popular taste, and Lautrec was swift to appreciate the outlet they offered to an artist anxious to make his name, but too diffident as yet to show his work to established exhibiting bodies. His first published work was a bar scene, *Le Gin Cocktail* (1886), which was followed by a series on Parisian life, and in 1889 he received a commission to prepare drawings from four of his most successful portraits for reproduction in the local journal *Le Courrier Français*.

The first of these, *The Hangover*, was a portrait of a young woman, shown in firm profile like so many of Lautrec's portraits, sitting melancholy and abstracted at a café table with a bottle and glass in front of her. The link with Degas's painting *In The Café (L'Absinthe)* of 1876, both conceptually and compositionally, is clear, but the effect is very different. Degas's self-absorbed drinker sits with hands folded and eyes downcast, the picture of female passivity, next to and yet detached from her male companion. Lautrec's model, sprawled confidently across the café table, chin on hand, is an altogether more characterful, positive and independent image. This reflects his knowledge of his subject, Suzanne Valadon, who had worked as a trapeze artist and bareback rider until injury forced her retirement. At this time she was working as a full-time artist's model, and for a while was Lautrec's lover. Her son Maurice Utrillo had been born in 1883.

Another painting reproduced in the *Courrier* showed Jeanne Wenz, sister of yet another fellow student at Cormon's. This was one of a series of four portraits of women painted between 1886 and 1888 which were intended to represent an area of Paris, hence its title *A La Bastille*. Its reproduction no doubt generated valuable publicity, but Lautrec was never paid by the *Courrier*'s editor and had to take legal action to get his work back. In revenge the *Courrier* published a damning obituary in September 1901, describing Lautrec as 'a sort of Quasimodo, whom nobody could look at without laughing . . . who did all he could to make the girls of Montmartre look ridiculous, base, slovenly, or trivially obscene.'

In the 1870s the simple cabarets and cafés with which Lautrec had become familiar as a student were developing into more ambitious places of entertainment, and the Moulin de la Galette, at the top of Montmartre's hill, was one of the earliest and most popular of these. As well as a café-restaurant in the grounds of the original mill, there was a dance floor, lit in the evening with gas lamps, and an orchestra. This was the subject for Lautrec's first large-scale dance scene, *A Dance at the Moulin de la Galette* (1889), and also provided him with his first models for the paintings and lithographs of professional singers and entertainers for which he is best known today. These were the dancer Louis Weber, known professionally as 'La Goulue', the glutton, and her partner Etienne Renaudin, called 'Le Désossé', the boneless one, for the fluidity of his dancing.

Another form of nocturnal leisure that developed above all in Montmartre was the *cabaret-chantant* or *cabaret-artistique*, where professional entertainers were the principal attraction. The Chat Noir, opened in 1882, was one of the first of these, and rapidly became the center of an iconoclastic group of writers and artists, with leanings towards Anarchism. One of the regular performers at the Chat Noir was Aristide Bruant, who was working as a clerk at the Gare St-Lazare when he was attracted to nearby Montparnasse and began writing and singing his own songs, devoted to extoling the life of the underworld and attacking the complacent tedium of bourgeois life. His success was such that he soon opened his own *cabaret-artistique*, the Mirliton, which he advertised as 'the place to visit if you want to be insulted.' Bruant also published his own journal, *Le Mirliton*, and it was the four cover illustrations that Lautrec produced for this in 1886-87, three of them colored in stencil from separate relief plates, that moved him to explore the potential of this apparently rigid technique, by using a very limited range of flat colors and concentrating on radical compositional effects. This in turn led to other forms of graphic art, introducing Lautrec to the medium in which he was to achieve his greatest fame.

Poster art had been a feature of Paris since the end of the eighteenth century, but had changed radically in the second half of the nineteenth due to a particular artist, Jules Chéret, and the mastery of improved lithographic techniques he acquired while working for a London publisher. On his return to Paris in 1866, he opened his own press and started to produce posters which, with their dramatic combination of typography and images, began a stylistic revolution. Some of his most famous designs were created for the Moulin Rouge, a hugely successful music hall it was from the Moulin Rouge in 1891 that Lautrec received his first poster commission.

There is a photograph of Lautrec with the Moulin Rouge manager, Charles Zidler, admiring an earlier Chéret poster for the music hall, and presumably Zidler had something similar in mind, but what Lautrec produced was quite different, both technically and compositionally. *Moulin Rouge: La Goulue*, rather than Chéret's generalized and busy depiction of a troop of diaphonously clad dancers riding on donkeys, focuses on two individuals, the attenuated figure of Valentin le Désossé in the foreground, dramatically cropped at waist level, and his partner La Goulue in the midground, swirling her petticoats in an energetic dance and outlined against the background audience, who are seen only in silhouette. Lautrec's original used a combination of media, including brushwork and chalk, and a scattering technique of spraying paint from a loaded brush through a sieve, which allowed rich mixtures of color.

The poster appeared in an edition of 3000 and was an immediate success, confirming Lautrec in the direction in which his work was anyway tending. He was particularly pleased with the acclaim of the critic Arsène Alexandre, one of the first proponents of the Impressionists, and was emboldened to exhibit the work both at the eighth Salon des Indépendants in Paris, and at the annual exhibition of Les XX in Brussels. Two poster commissions from Aristide Bruant, as a result probably the most recognizable entertainer in history, followed almost at once, and inspired Lautrec's friend and patron Thadée Natanson, by now proprietor of the influential journal *La Revue Blanche*, to write:

The posters that have burst forth on the walls of Paris, or are still adorning them, have surprised, disturbed and delighted us. The black crowd teeming round the dancer with her skirts tucked up, and her astonishing partner in the foreground, and the masterful portrait of Aristide Bruant are equally unforgettable.

It was a good moment for Lautrec to embark on graphic work; the burgeoning middle classes were beginning to take an interest in affordable art, and posters were particularly popular, with at least four galleries dealing in them almost exclusively. The music hall was not the only source of employment; Lautrec was also commissioned to produce theater posters, which in turn introduced him to the more mainstream and fashionable world of the boulevards. It is clear that Lautrec's graphic art was far more profitable for him than his painting, and it has tended to be preferred to his painting, both at the time and since.

One of the most characteristic features of Lautrec's art from the beginning, and which became a definitive element in his graphic work, was his interest in, sometimes almost obsession with, particular individuals. Of these Jane Avril, the illegitimate daughter of a noted Second Empire courtesan, was perhaps the most significant, in both paint and poster. In portraits, Lautrec represented her as a solitary, introspective character, and this mood spills over into at least one of the posters of her, *Divan Japonais* (1893), which also features the curiously cropped figure of the singer Yvette Guilbert, another of Lautrec's favorite models. The series of images of *Jane Avril Dancing*, however, show a very different side of her personality in her frenzied and abandoned dance routines.

The element of exaggeration and distortion that was almost an inevitable characteristic of late nineteenth-century graphic art, with its limited technical repertoire, appealed to the caricaturist in Lautrec, and some of his representations are far less sympathetic to their subject. Yvette Guilbert protested of his half-mocking, half-affectionate lithograph *Yvette Guilbert Taking a Curtain Call* (1894) that he had made her a monster, while *Reine de Joie* (1892) is a savagely unsparing depiction of a calculating prostitute and her bloated admirer.

It was to the world of prostitution that Lautrec turned his attention in the 1890s, reflecting the established and accepted role of brothels in contemporary Paris society, already celebrated in fictional form, for example in Emile Zola's novel *Nana*. Lautrec's predilection for brothel life – he became a favored lodger in the magnificent establishment in the rue des Moulins, sharing the prostitutes' meals after the clientele had gone and working the mechanical piano while they danced – has caused greater controversy since. It has led to the suggestion that his interest in prostitutes was motivated rather by the dominant ideology of the time, the simplistic and patronizing view of woman as either wife or whore, than by any social concern. Certainly Lautrec, unlike Zola, was no reformer, but his depictions of life in the rue des Moulins contain none of the dehumanizing contempt shown by, for instance, Degas or Forain, nor are they, on the whole, overtly sentimental or erotic. They focus rather on the mundane routine of communal life, the tedium of the hours spent waiting for custom (*The Salon at the Rue des Moulins*) or the nervousness of the expectant customer (*Monsieur, Madame and a Dog*), while the lesbianism that was common in brothels provoked some of his most tender, graceful and affectionate work (*L'Abandon or Two Friends*).

In the later 1890s Lautrec's painting also achieved a greater degree of popularity, coinciding ironically with the onset of the physical decline, due to alcoholism and probably syphilis, which was to kill him. The paintings of this period, such as *The Milliner*, are more painterly than his earlier work, more concerned with subtle brushwork and tone, used to convey the sensitivity of his observation.

The departure of Lautrec's mother, the Comtesse Adèle, from Paris early in 1899 seems to have precipitated a crisis both in his drinking and in his health, and he was compulsorily confined for a few months at a detoxification clinic near Neuilly. On his release he went on a succession of visits to friends, as part of a benign conspiracy to prevent him drinking, but in September 1901 he collapsed again, was removed to the family home by his mother, and died within a few days. His father, who was present at his deathbed, described him, in a letter written to Princeteau the following day, as 'the kindest soul you could ever have met.'

Below
Moulin Rouge: La Goulue, a lithograph in four colors, was Lautrec's first poster; it appeared on the streets of Paris in October 1891 and brought him overnight success. With its simplification of form and novel typographical repetitions, this image greatly extended the visual language of the poster.

THE YOUNG ROUTY AT CÉLEYRAN, 1882
Oil on canvas, 24⅛ × 19¾ inches (61 × 50 cm)
Musée d'Albi

WOMAN SEATED ON A DIVAN, 1883
Oil on canvas, 21⅝ × 18⅛ inches (55 × 46 cm)
Musée d'Albi

Dancer in her Dressing Room, 1885
Fresco transferred to canvas, 45¼ × 39¾ inches
(115 × 101 cm)
Private Collection

PORTRAIT OF VINCENT VAN GOGH, 1887
Pastel on board, 22½ × 18⅜ inches (57 × 46.5 cm)
Vincent van Gogh Foundation/Vincent van Gogh Museum,
Amsterdam

The Hangover or the Drinker, 1888/89
Oil and black crayon (or chalk) on canvas,
18½ × 21¾ inches (47.1 × 55.5 cm)
*Harvard University Art Museums, Bequest of the
Collection of Maurice Wertheim, class of 1906*

15

Left
MONSIEUR SAMARY AT THE COMÉDIE FRANCAISE, 1889
Oil on board, 29½ × 20½ inches (75 × 52 cm)
Musée d'Orsay, Paris

Above
MONSIEUR DÉSIRÉ DIHAU,
BASSOONIST OF THE OPÉRA, 1890
Oil on board, 22⅛ × 17¾ inches (56 × 45 cm)
Musée d'Albi

17

AT THE MOULIN ROUGE:
THE DANCE, 1890
Oil on canvas, 45½ × 59 inches
(115 × 150 cm)
Philadelphia Museum of Art,
the Henry P McIlhenny Collection

18

Above
LA TOILETTE, 1889/90/91
Oil on board, 24¼ × 20½ inches (64 × 52 cm)
Musée d'Orsay, Paris

Right
WOMAN SEATED IN THE GARDEN OF MONSIEUR FOREST:
JUSTINE DIEUHL, 1891
Oil on board, 29¼ × 22⅞ inches (75 × 58 cm)
Musée d'Orsay, Paris

20

74

AT THE MOULIN ROUGE, 1892-95
Oil on canvas, 48½ × 55⅜ inches (123 × 141 cm)
*The Art Institute of Chicago, Helen Birch Bartlett
Memorial Collection, 1928.610*

Above
A CORNER OF THE MOULIN DE LA GALETTE, 1892
Oil on cardboard on wood, 39½ × 35⅛ inches
(100 × 89 cm)
National Gallery of Art, Washington,
Chester Dale Collection

Right
AMBASSADEURS: ARISTIDE BRUANT, 1892
Brush and spatter lithograph in five colors on two sheets of
paper, 53¹⁵⁄₁₆ × 37⅜ inches (137 × 95 cm)
San Diego Museum of Art, California, Gift of the Baldwin
M Baldwin Foundation

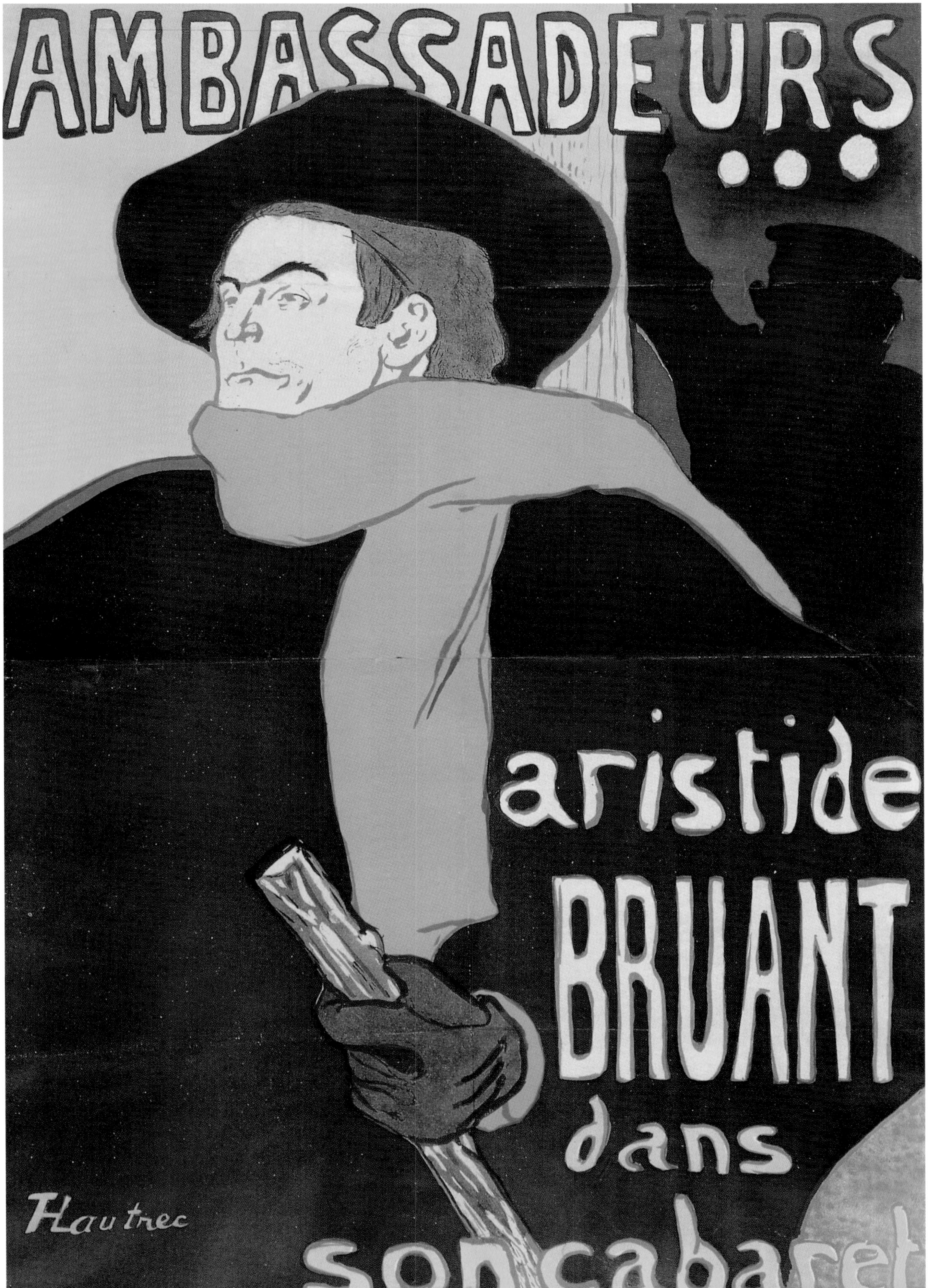
AMBASSADEURS
aristide
BRUANT
dans
son cabaret
HLautrec

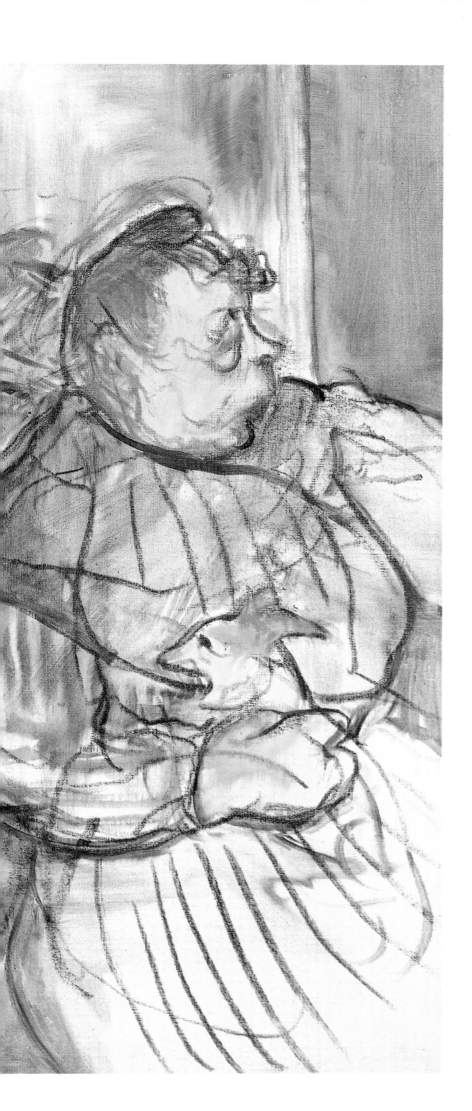

MONSIEUR, MADAME AND THE DOG, 1893
Oil on canvas, 19 × 23⅝ inches (48 × 60 cm)
Musée d'Albi

33

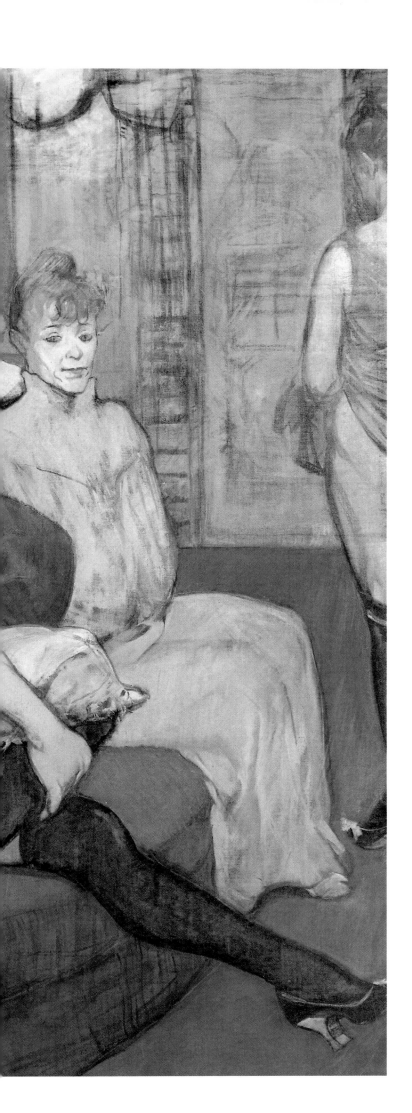

THE SALON AT THE RUE DES MOULINS, 1894
Oil on canvas, 44 × 52¼ inches (111.5 × 132.5 cm)
Musée d'Albi

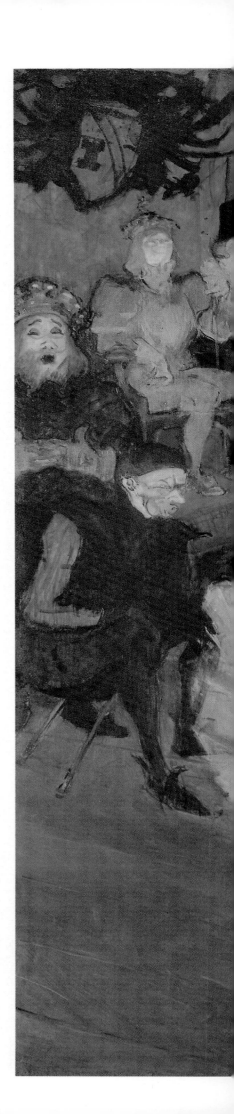

Marcelle Lender Dancing the Bolero in 'Chilperic', 1895
Oil on canvas, 57⅛ × 59 inches (145 × 150 cm)
National Gallery of Art, Washington

May Belfort

Left
NAPOLEON, 1895
Lithograph on paper, 23¹⁵⁄₁₆ × 18⅛ inches (59.3 × 46 cm)
Private Collection

Above
MISS MAY BELFORT, 1895
Brush, spatter and crayon lithograph, 31 × 23⅝ inches
(79.4 × 60.4 cm)
British Museum, London

39

MISIA NATANSON PLAYING THE PIANO, 1897
Oil on board glued to wood panel, 32 × 37½ inches
(82 × 96 cm)
Kunstmuseum, Berne

41

ACKNOWLEDGMENTS

The publisher would like to thank Martin Bristow for designing this book, and the following institutions and agencies for permission to reproduce photographic material.

The Art Institute of Chicago: pages 24-25
Bibliothèque Nationale, Paris: page 9
British Museum, London: page 39
Harvard University Art Museums: pages 14-15
Kunstmuseum, Berne: pages 40-41
Musée d'Albi: pages 10, 11, 17, 32-33, 34-35, 43

Musée d'Orsay, Paris/photo courtesy of Réunion des Musées nationaux: pages 16, 20, 21, 22
National Gallery of Art, Washington: pages 26, 36-37
Oskar Reinhart Collection, Winterthur: page 42
Philadelphia Museum of Art: pages 18-19
Private collection: pages 12, 31, 38
San Diego Museum of Art, California: pages 27, 28, 29, 30
Toledo Museum of Art, Toledo: page 23
Vincent van Gogh Foundation/Vincent van Gogh Museum, Amsterdam: page 13